Taking the Tests

Your child should record their answers in the Answer Sheets booklet provided – not in the test booklet. Answer Sheets are provided for all three tests in this pack.

The actual 11+ test will be marked by a computer, but you will need to score the practice tests yourself using the Answer Key in this booklet. It is important for your child to learn how to use the Answer Sheets properly, in preparation for the real test: they should record an answer in the appropriate box by drawing a clear line through it with a pencil. Mistakes should be rubbed out carefully and **not** crossed out, since in the actual test this would not be recorded correctly by the computer. You can ignore the boxes at the top marked 'Pupil Number', 'School Number' and 'Date of Birth'. These need to be filled in only for the actual test. By encountering these features now, your child will be more familiar with the style of the actual 11+ paper when they take the test.

Timing a Test

It is useful for your child to practise taking tests under timed conditions. Allow them 50 minutes for a test, but do not start timing until they have read all the instructions and/or filled in all the details at the top of the Answer Sheet.

If they have not finished at the end of 50 minutes, draw a line underneath the question they are on, or draw a ring around its number, and then let them carry on. When you mark the test, you will be able to see how many questions your child got right in the allocated time and how many questions overall. This will give you a good indication of whether they need to develop their speed and/or work more accurately.

Marking and Feedback

The answers are provided on pages 4–6. Only these answers are allowed. One mark should be given for each correct answer – do not allow half marks or 'the benefit of the doubt'. Do not deduct marks for wrong answers.

The results may suggest that more practice is needed. Always try to be positive and encouraging. Talk through the mistakes your child has made in a constructive way. Work out together how to get the right answer.

Answer Key

Practice Paper 1

Question	Answer	Question	Answer	Question	Answer
1	15	21	D	41	$16\,cm^3$
2	98	22	$(3, 1\frac{1}{2})$	42	E
3	a bucket	23	C	43	0.98
4	212	24	30	44	A
5	40	25	4	45	4.1
6	£15.58	26	8.28	46	78°
7	Edinburgh	27	6	47	10
8	8, 12, 16	28	80	48	120°
9	I	29	9	49	−185
10	22	30	C	50	675 litres
11	95p	31	135		
12	£1.04	32	E		
13	56	33	25%		
14	160	34	D		
15	cricket, football, rugby	35	£10.00		
16	41 200	36	40%		
17	£6.23	37	1.7 m		
18	kite	38	3		
19	25	39	$16\,m^2$		
20	15 m	40	4		

Notes and Answers for Parents

Mathematics
Pack 1

Introduction

About the Tests

These tests are designed to give your child practice in sitting a formal type of examination before they take the actual 11+ test.

The papers are presented in a very similar way to many of the test papers used for selection at 11+, and the questions represent the type of questions used, although they may not be exactly the same level of difficulty. Therefore, your child's scores on these tests will not necessarily be a direct indication of their likely score on an actual 11+ test. Furthermore, the pass marks for the actual test will depend, to some extent, on the overall standard of the candidates.

Preparation for Testing

Give your child the test at an appropriate time, when they are both physically and mentally alert. Choose a suitable area for them to work in – make sure they can work comfortably and are free from any distractions.

Before your child takes a practice test, discuss with them the reasons why they are doing the test. Also, explain that they might find some of the questions difficult, but that they should work as quickly and as carefully as they can. If they get stuck on a question, they should not waste too much time on it but move on to the next one. If they have time left at the end, they can go back to it then.

Answer Key

Practice Paper 2

Question	Answer	Question	Answer	Question	Answer
1	90	21	37 m	41	²⁄₅ of 75
2	75	22	A	42	D
3	8	23	32	43	kite
4	14	24	£18.50	44	22
5	29p	25	5	45	990
6	2.03 m	26	40%	46	340
7	28	27	−3 °C	47	55°
8	MUM	28	£5.25	48	8.5 m²
9	£825	29	28 m	49	B
10	(4 , 3)	30	9.4 kg	50	12
11	16	31	13.5 cm²		
12	9 cm	32	isosceles		
13	111	33	43		
14	3	34	3 °C		
15	6.5	35	3		
16	800 ml	36	B		
17	1	37	5 seconds		
18	60	38	isosceles, scalene, equilateral		
19	12	39	E		
20	£8.05	40	D (2 , 3) E (4 , 8) F (7 , 5)		

Answer Key

Practice Paper 3

Question	Answer		Question	Answer		Question	Answer
1	300		21	£5.74		41	25.5 m²
2	15		22	250 miles		42	C
3	24 706		23	£738		43	£1695
4	174		24	regular hexagon		44	(3 , 7)
5	0.02		25	£2018.14		45	£7.60
6	3 kg		26	B + A + F		46	24
7	42		27	80 000 mm		47	A
8	108		28	Q and S		48	5000 cm²
9	54		29	5		49	D
10	8 cm²		30	6.6 m		50	1.5 cm
11	27		31	$\frac{1}{2}$			
12	7 °C		32	132			
13	8, 27, 64		33	C			
14	$\frac{10}{12}$		34	B			
15	38		35	$\frac{5}{8}$			
16	TOT		36	rectangle			
17	12		37	210°			
18	P (1 , 3) Q (4 , 6)		38	25 800			
	R (7 , 2)		39	$\frac{3}{8}$			
19	150°		40	72 km			
20	(3 , 7)						

Published by GL Assessment, 1st Floor, Vantage London, Great West Road, Brentford TW8 9AG.

Printed in China.

Code 6802 009
1(11.18) PF

Answer Sheets

Maths
Practice Papers 1–3

This booklet contains the answer sheets needed for Maths Practice Papers 1–3.

Please make sure you use the correct answer sheet for the test being taken, following the title at the top of each page.

The following answer sheets are included:

Maths Practice Paper 1
Maths Practice Paper 2
Maths Practice Paper 3

11+ Practice Papers

GL Assessment®

Published by GL Assessment, 1st Floor, Vantage London, Great West Road, Brentford TW8 9AG.

Printed in China.

Code 6802 010
1(11.18) PF

GL Assessment®

Pupil's Name: Aanya
School Name: Frithwood Primary School

DATE OF TEST

Day	Month	Year
1 7	0 2	2 5

UNIQUE PUPIL NUMBER

SCHOOL NUMBER

DATE OF BIRTH

Day	Month	Year
2 4	0 2	1 5

Please mark boxes with a thin horizontal line like this ▬.

1
10 / 15 ✓ / 20 / 25 / 36

2
100 / 102 / 108 / 90 / 98 ✓

3
a teapot / a bucket ✓ / a milk bottle / a teacup / a teaspoon

4
203 / 106 / 309 / 159 / 212 ✓

5
5 / 25 / 32 / 40 ✓ / 55

6
£16.68 / £15.68 / £16.42 / £15.58 ✓ / £16.02

7
Manchester / Glasgow / York / Edinburgh ✓ / Newcastle

8
8, 9, 10 / 9, 10, 12 / 8, 12, 16 ✓ / 12, 14, 16 / 14, 15, 16

9
I / K / U / Y / W

10
44 / 18 / 22 ✓ / 6 / 32

11
96p / 85p / 86p / 95p ✓ / 30p

12
£0.82 / £1.04 ✓ / £1.20 / £1.40 / £1.02

13
57 / 59 / 52 / 54 / 56 ✓

14
5760 / 160 ✓ / 120 / 320 / 954

15
swimming, volleyball, rowing / swimming, football, rowing / cricket, football, rugby ✓ / cricket, volleyball, rowing / swimming, football, rugby

16
512 / 40 012 / 41 200 ✓ / 41 012 / 4120

17
£7.83 / 96p / £5.63 / £6.23 ✓ / £6.41

18
parallelogram / kite ✓ / trapezium / rhombus / rectangle

19
21 / 20 / 23 / 26 / 25 ✓

20
15m ✓ / 6m / 18m / 9m / 12m

21
A / B / C / D ✓ / E

22
(1, 3) / (3, 1½) ✓ / (3, 1) / (1½, 3) / (3½, 1½)

23
A / B ✓ / C / D / E

24
33 ✓ / 36 / 27 / 48 / 30

25
2 / 4 ✓ / 6 / 8 / 16

26
8.80 / 8.29 / 8.26 / 8.28 ✓ / 8.08

27
6 / 5 / 4 / 2 / 3 ✓

28
100 / 40 / 50 / 80. ✓ / 25

29
15 / 3 / 9 ✓ / 12 / 6

30
A / B / C ✓ / D / E

31
178 / 135 ✓ / 133 / 81 / 82

32
A / B / C / D / E ✓

33
12% / 3% / 30% / 25% ✓ / 30%

34
A / B / C / D ✓ / E

35
£9.00 / £10.00 / £11.00 / £12.00 / £13.00

36
40% ✓ / 24% / 30% / 20% / 48%

37
1.3m / 1.4m / 2m / 1.6m / 1.7m ✓

38
3 ✓ / 6 / 7 / 8 / 10

39
13m² / 18.5m² / 15m² / 21m² / 16m² ✓

40
7 / 4 / 0 / 2 / 5

41
32cm³ / 48cm³ / 24cm³ / 14cm³ / 16cm³ ✓

42
A / B / C / D / E

43
1.1 / 0.98 ✓ / 0.9 / 1.09 / 1.9

44
A / B / C / D / E

45
4.1 / 4.3 / 4.13 / 5.13 / 4.2

46
71° / 26° / 78° ✓ / 54° / 66°

47
12 / 20 / 6 / 10 / 14

48
100° / 130° / 105° / 120° / 110°

49
−175 / −69 / −185 / −59 / −101

50
625 litres ✓ / 375 litres / 525 litres / 270 litres / 675 litres

45/50 = 90%

GL Assessment®

Pupil's Name: Aanya Karia
School Name:

DATE OF TEST
Day	Month	Year
1 8	0 2	2 5

DATE OF BIRTH
Day	Month	Year
2 4	0 2	(crossed out)

1 5

UNIQUE PUPIL NUMBER

SCHOOL NUMBER

Please mark boxes with a thin horizontal line like this ▬.

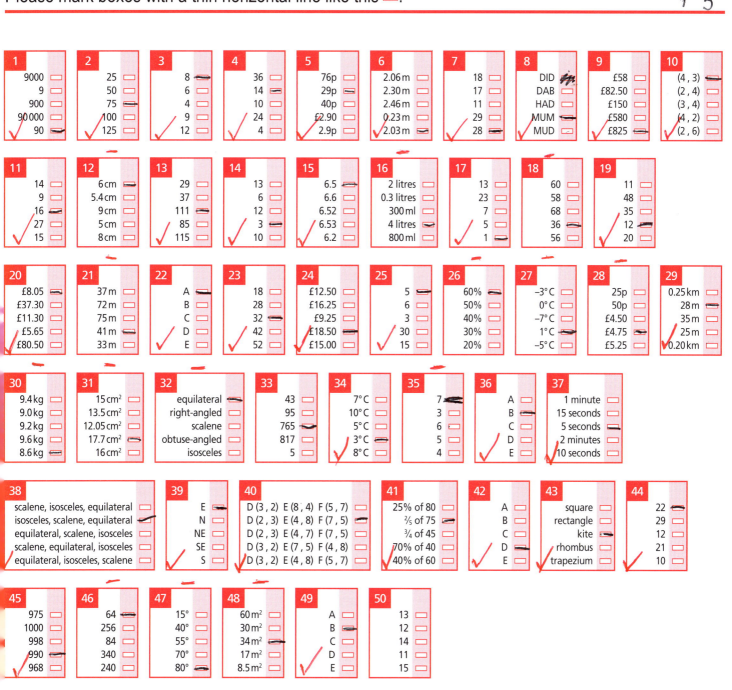

1	9000 · 9 · 900 · 90 000 · 90 ✓
2	25 · 50 · 75 · 100 · 125 ✓
3	8 · 6 · 4 · 9 · 12 ✓
4	36 · 14 · 10 · 24 · 4 ✓
5	76p · 29p · 40p · £2.90 · 2.9p ✓
6	2.06 m · 2.30 m · 2.46 m · 0.23 m · 2.03 m ✓
7	18 · 17 · 11 · 29 · 28 ✓
8	DID · DAB · HAD · MUM · MUD ✓
9	£58 · £82.50 · £150 · £580 · £825
10	(4, 3) · (2, 4) · (3, 4) · (4, 2) · (2, 6) ✓
11	14 · 9 · 16 · 27 ✓ · 15
12	6 cm · 5.4 cm · 9 cm · 5 cm · 8 cm
13	29 · 37 · 111 · 85 · 115 ✓
14	13 · 6 · 12 · 3 · 10 ✓
15	6.5 · 6.6 · 6.52 · 6.53 · 6.2
16	2 litres · 0.3 litres · 300 ml · 4 litres · 800 ml
17	13 · 23 · 7 · 5 · 1 ✓
18	60 · 58 · 68 · 36 · 56
19	11 · 48 · 35 · 12 · 20 ✓
20	£8.05 · £37.30 · £11.30 · £5.65 · £80.50
21	37 m · 72 m · 75 m · 41 m · 33 m
22	A · B · C · D ✓ · E
23	18 · 28 · 32 · 42 · 52 ✓
24	£12.50 · £16.25 · £9.25 · £18.50 · £15.00 ✓
25	5 · 6 · 3 · 30 · 15 ✓
26	60% · 50% · 40% · 30% · 20%
27	−3°C · 0°C · −7°C · 1°C · −5°C
28	25p · 50p · £4.50 · £4.75 · £5.25
29	0.25 km · 28 m · 35 m · 25 m · 0.20 km ✓
30	9.4 kg · 9.0 kg · 9.2 kg · 9.6 kg · 8.6 kg
31	15 cm² · 13.5 cm² · 12.05 cm² · 17.7 cm² · 16 cm²
32	equilateral · right-angled · scalene · obtuse-angled · isosceles
33	43 · 95 · 765 · 817 · 5
34	7°C · 10°C · 5°C · 3°C ✓ · 8°C
35	7 · 3 · 6 · 5 · 4
36	A · B · C · D ✓ · E
37	1 minute · 15 seconds · 5 seconds · 2 minutes · 10 seconds ✓
38	scalene, isosceles, equilateral · isosceles, scalene, equilateral ✓ · equilateral, scalene, isosceles · scalene, equilateral, isosceles · equilateral, isosceles, scalene
39	E · N · NE · SE · S ✓
40	D (3, 2) E (8, 4) F (5, 7) · D (2, 3) E (4, 8) F (7, 5) ✓ · D (2, 3) E (4, 7) F (7, 5) · D (3, 2) E (7, 5) F (4, 8) · D (3, 2) E (4, 8) F (5, 7)
41	25% of 80 · ⅖ of 75 · ¾ of 45 · 70% of 40 · 40% of 60 ✓
42	A · B · C · D ✓ · E
43	square · rectangle · kite · rhombus · trapezium
44	22 · 29 · 12 · 21 · 10 ✓
45	975 · 1000 · 998 · 990 · 968 ✓
46	64 · 256 · 84 · 340 · 240
47	15° · 40° · 55° · 70° · 80°
48	60 m² · 30 m² · 34 m² · 17 m² · 8.5 m²
49	A · B · C · D ✓ · E
50	13 · 12 · 14 · 11 · 15

34/50 = 68%

MATHS PRACTICE PAPER 3

GL Assessment®

| Pupil's Name | Aanya |
| School Name | Karia |

DATE OF TEST

Day	Month	Year
1 9	0 2	2 5

UNIQUE PUPIL NUMBER

SCHOOL NUMBER

DATE OF BIRTH

Day	Month	Year
2 4	0 2	1 5

Please mark boxes with a thin horizontal line like this ▬.

1
- 3000
- 30
- 12 300
- 3
- 300 ✓

2
- 3
- 15
- 10
- 25
- 30 ✓

3
- 24 706
- 2476
- 24 760
- 2470.6
- 24 700.6 ✓

4
- 87
- 169
- 435
- 174
- 56 ✓

5
- 1.01
- 0.99
- 0.02
- 1.25
- 0.5 ✓

6
- 3 kg
- 300 g
- 30 kg
- 300 kg
- 3 g ✓

7
- 84
- 42
- 82
- 48
- 36 ✓

8
- 286
- 108
- 464
- 180
- 414 ✓

9
- 45
- 48
- 50
- 60
- 54 ✓

10
- 20 cm²
- 16 cm²
- 8 cm²
- 2 cm²
- 4 cm² ✓

11
- 27
- 5
- 9
- 4½
- 24 ✓

12
- 1°C
- −1°C
- 7°C
- −7°C
- −4°C ✓

13
- 8, 16, 32 ✓
- 8, 27, 64
- 16, 32, 64
- 9, 27, 64
- 5, 25, 125

14
- ½
- ¾
- ⅝
- ¹⁰⁄₁₂ ✓
- ⁴⁄₆

15
- 38
- 19
- 33
- 21 ✓
- 39

16
- TOT
- ON
- BIB
- OF
- BE ✓

17
- 6
- 18
- 12
- 2
- 5 ✓

18
- P (3 , 1) Q (6 , 4) R (2 , 7)
- P (1 , 2) Q (4 , 6) R (7 , 1)
- P (1 , 3) Q (4 , 6) R (7 , 2)
- P (1 , 3) Q (7 , 2) R (4 , 6)
- P (1 , 3) Q (4 , 6) R (2 , 7) ✓

19
- 135°
- 155°
- 150° ✓
- 165°
- 130°

20
- (7 , 3)
- (4 , 6)
- (2 , 7)
- (3 , 7)
- (4 , 7) ✓

21
- £5.60
- £2.05
- £6.04
- £4.92
- £5.74 ✓

22 ✗
- 250 miles
- 25 miles
- 205 miles
- 800 miles
- 40 miles

23
- £492
- £205
- £287
- £246
- £738

24
- kite
- regular pentagon
- regular hexagon
- rhombus
- regular octagon ✓

25
- £1478.39
- £1723.39
- £1773.14
- £1878.39
- £2018.14 ✓

26
- B + A + F
- G − B − F
- F + C + B
- A + B + D
- F + A + B + A

27
- 8 mm
- 80 mm
- 800 mm
- 8000 mm
- 80 000 mm

28
- P and R
- Q and S
- R and T
- P and S
- P and Q ✓

29
- 5
- 6
- 7
- 8 ✓
- 9

30
- 25.2 m
- 6.6 m
- 9.0 m
- 11.4 m
- 5.4 m ✓

31
- ½
- ⅔
- ¼
- ⅗ ✓
- ³⁄₉

32
- 108
- 132
- 96
- 120 ✓
- 84

33
- A
- B
- C
- D ✓
- E

34
- A
- B
- C
- D ✓
- E

35
- ⅝
- ¹²⁄₁₆
- ⁴⁄₁₀
- ⁶⁄₈
- ⁸⁄₅ ✓

36
- rectangle
- trapezium
- kite
- rhombus
- square

37
- 90°
- 150°
- 180°
- 210°
- 270° ✓

38
- 2580
- 28 500
- 386
- 258
- 25 800 ✓

39
- ⅔
- ⁶⁄₈
- ²⁄₄₅
- ¾
- ⅜ ✓

40
- 40 km
- 56 km
- 72 km
- 88 km
- 104 km ✓

41
- 24 m²
- 30 m²
- 29 m²
- 25.5 m²
- 22.5 m² ✓

42
- A
- B
- C
- D
- E ✓

43
- £1380
- £1320
- £1815
- £1695 ✓
- £1440

44
- (3 , 4)
- (3 , 7)
- (5 , 2)
- (8 , 3) ✓
- (8 , 7)

45
- £1.90
- £7.50
- £7.60
- £8.55
- £9.30

46
- 6
- 18
- 20
- 24 ✓
- 30

47
- A
- B
- C ✓
- D
- E

48
- 50 cm²
- 500 cm²
- 5000 cm²
- 2500 cm²
- 250 cm²

49
- A
- B
- C
- D ✓
- E

50
- 6.0 cm
- 5.5 cm
- 4.0 cm
- 2.0 cm
- 1.5 cm ✓

45/50 = 90%

34/50 — 68%

11+MA-3

END OF TEST

Practice Paper 1

Mathematics

Read the following carefully:

1. **Do not open or turn over the page in this booklet until you are told to do so.**

2. This is a multiple-choice test in which you have to mark your answer to each question on the separate answer sheet. You should mark only one answer for each question.

3. Draw a firm line clearly through the rectangle next to your answer like this ⟺. If you make a mistake, rub it out as completely as you can and put in your new answer.

4. Be sure to keep your place on the answer sheet. Mark your answer in the box that has the same number as the question.

5. You may not be able to finish all the questions, but try to do as many as you can. If you cannot do a question, **do not waste time on it but go on to the next**. If you are not sure of an answer, choose the one you think is best.

6. You may do any rough working on a separate sheet of paper.

7. **Work as quickly and as carefully as you can.**

8. You will have **50 minutes** to do the test.

1 Uplands School did a survey on favourite fruit juice flavours.

Favourite fruit juice flavour	
Key: ⊔ stands for 10 children	
⊏ stands for 5 children	
Orange	⊔ ⊔ ⊔ ⊏
Apple	⊔ ⊔
Grapefruit	⊔ ⊔ ⊔ ⊔ ⊏
Blackcurrant	⊔ ⊔ ⊔ ⊔
Pineapple	⊔ ⊏

How many children liked pineapple flavour best?

A 10   B 15   C 20   D 25   E 35

2 There are 360 children at Hilltop School.
262 children walk to school. The rest travel by bus or car.

How many children travel by bus or car?

A 100   B 102   C 108   D 90   E 98

3 **Which container will hold about 5 litres?**

A   a teapot
B   a bucket
C   a milk bottle
D   a teacup
E   a teaspoon

4

In 2015, 53 children went on a school trip.
In 2016, twice as many went as in 2015.
In 2017, twice as many went as in 2016.

How many children went in 2017?

A 203   B 106   C 309   D 159   E 212

5

Which number is divisible by both 5 and 10?

A 5   B 25   C 32   D 40   E 55

6

Mr Miller's supermarket bill is £17.03.
At the checkout, he uses some vouchers to reduce his bill by £1.45.

What is the new amount he has to pay?

A £16.68   B £15.68   C £16.42   D £15.58   E £16.02

7

A newspaper showed temperatures in 12 cities on a day in December:

London 5 °C	Glasgow –3 °C
Newcastle –6 °C	Birmingham 4 °C
Cardiff 6 °C	Edinburgh –7 °C
Leicester 3 °C	Leeds –4 °C
Southampton 7 °C	Manchester –1 °C
Liverpool 2 °C	York –5 °C

Which was the coldest?

A   Manchester
B   Glasgow
C   York
D   Edinburgh
E   Newcastle

8 Which answer has three numbers that are all multiples of 3 or 4?

A 8, 9, 10

B 9, 10, 12

C 8, 12, 16

D 12, 14, 16

E 14, 15, 16

9 Which of the five large letters has TWO lines of symmetry?

I K U Y W

A I   B K   C U   D Y   E W

10 Sarah collected the following data during a survey of her friends.

	Favourite Subject		
	Science	Maths	English
Boys	28	6	14
Girls	20	?	10

100 pupils completed the survey.

How many girls gave Maths as their favourite subject?

A 44   B 18   C 22   D 6   E 32

11

I bought 8 small packets of sweets.
I was given £2.40 change from £10.

How much did each packet cost?

A 96p   B 85p   C 86p   D 95p   E 30p

12

Ranjit has a 50 pence piece, two 20 pence pieces, a 10 pence piece and two 2 pence pieces.

How much money does he have?

A £0.82   B £1.04   C £1.20   D £1.40   E £1.02

13

This machine doubles and then adds 2.

? → 114

Which number has been put in?

A 57   B 59   C 52   D 54   E 56

14

School books are being packed in separate parcels, each one containing 6 books.

How many parcels are needed for 960 books?

A 5760   B 160   C 120   D 320   E 954

15

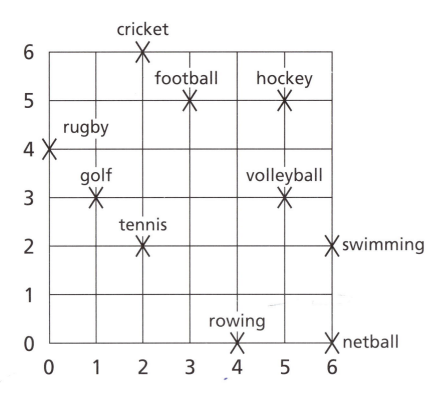

Name the sports at these coordinates:

(2 , 6), (3 , 5), (0 , 4)

A   swimming, volleyball, rowing

B   swimming, football, rowing

C   cricket, football, rugby

D   cricket, volleyball, rowing

E   swimming, football, rugby

16

A gardener looks after 100 flower beds.
She plants 412 bulbs in each bed.

How many bulbs does she plant?

A 512   B 40 012   C 41 200   D 41 012   E 4120

17 Batteries cost 89p each.

6
89
× 7
―――
623

How much will 7 batteries cost?

A £7.83

B 96p

C £5.63

Ⓓ £6.23

E £6.41

18 Tom has drawn a triangle.
He reflects it in the mirror line.

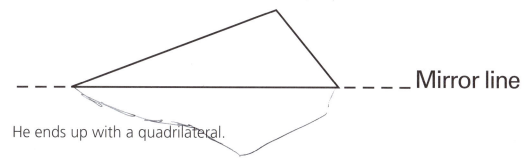 Mirror line

He ends up with a quadrilateral.

What type of quadrilateral is it?

A parallelogram

Ⓑ kite

C trapezium

D rhombus

E rectangle

19

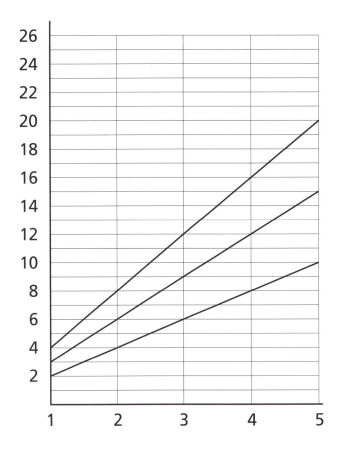

This graph shows multiplication tables.
The three lines shown start at 2, 3 and 4.

If a line starts at 5, what height will it reach on the y-axis?

A 21   B 20   C 23   D 26   E 25

20

Paul draws a plan of his school using a scale of 2 cm to 5 m.
On the plan, the school hall is 6 cm long.

What is the real length of the hall?

A 15 m   B 6 m   C 18 m   D 9 m   E 12 m

21

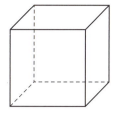
cube
A

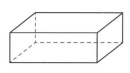
cuboid
B

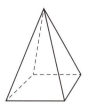
square-based
pyramid
C

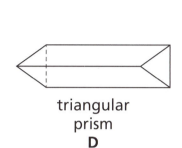
triangular
prism
D

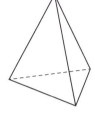
triangular
pyramid
E

Which solid shape has 5 faces and 9 edges?

A A   **B** B   **C** C   **D** D ✓   **E** E

---

22   This graph shows a sports ground.

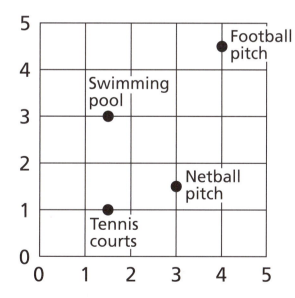

Where is the netball pitch?

A (1 , 3)   **B** (3 , 1½)   **C** (3 , 1)   **D** (1½ , 3)   **E** (3½ , 1½)

23

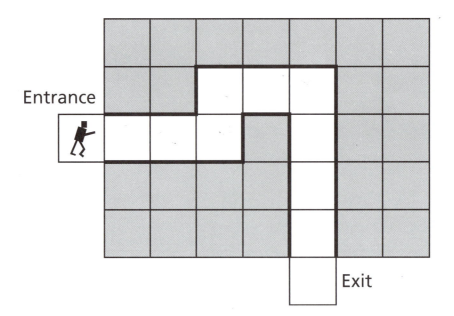

Balbir wants to guide a robot along the white squares through this maze.

The robot starts on the square marked 'Entrance' and must finish on the square marked 'Exit'.

It can only move FORWARD, TURN RIGHT 90° and TURN LEFT 90°.

Which instructions will guide the robot through the maze?

A FORWARD 4, TURN LEFT 90°, FORWARD 2, TURN RIGHT 90°,
   FORWARD 3, TURN RIGHT 90°, FORWARD 5.

B FORWARD 3, TURN RIGHT 90°, FORWARD 1, TURN RIGHT 90°,
   FORWARD 3, TURN LEFT 90°, FORWARD 3.

C FORWARD 3, TURN LEFT 90°, FORWARD 1, TURN RIGHT 90°,
   FORWARD 2, TURN RIGHT 90°, FORWARD 4.

D FORWARD 3, TURN RIGHT 90°, FORWARD 1, TURN LEFT 90°,
   FORWARD 2, TURN LEFT 90°, FORWARD 4.

E FORWARD 3, TURN LEFT 90°, FORWARD 1, TURN RIGHT 90°,
   FORWARD 3, TURN RIGHT 90°, FORWARD 4.

24

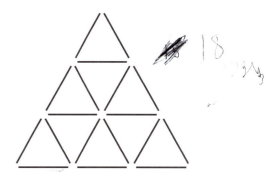

How many matchsticks are needed altogether to make the next shape in this sequence?

A 33 **B** 36 **C** 27 **D** 48 **E** 30

25

You multiply a number by itself.
The answer is then multiplied by the number you started with.
The new number is 64.

What number did you start with?

A 2 **B** 4 **C** 6 **D** 8 **E** 16

26

Look at this number line.

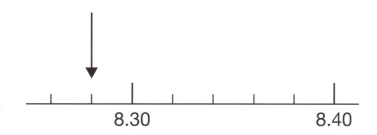

8.30   8.40

What number does the arrow point to?

A 8.80 **B** 8.29 **C** 8.26 **D** 8.28 **E** 8.08

27

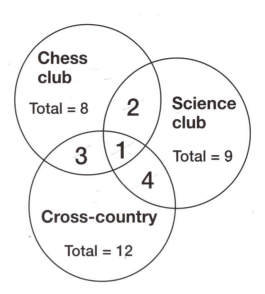

Chess club
Total = 8

Science club
Total = 9

Cross-country
Total = 12

2

3 1

4

24 children in a class are asked what activities they do.

How many do no activities?

A 6   **B** 5   **C** 4   **D** 2   **E** 3

28

There are 200 pupils at a school sports day.

²/₅ of them run in the relay race.

How many pupils is this?

A 100   **B** 40   **C** 50   **D** 80   **E** 25

29

This is a 'magic square' where the numbers in the rows and columns follow a logical sequence.

3	6	9
6	?	12
9	12	15

What is the missing number?

A 15   **B** 3   **C** 9   **D** 12   **E** 6

30

If the above angles were arranged in order of size, which would be in the middle?

A A   B B   C C   D D   E E

31

Iva plants 216 seedlings.

$\frac{3}{8}$ are killed by the frost.

How many seedlings survive?

A 178   B 135   C 133   D 81   E 82

32

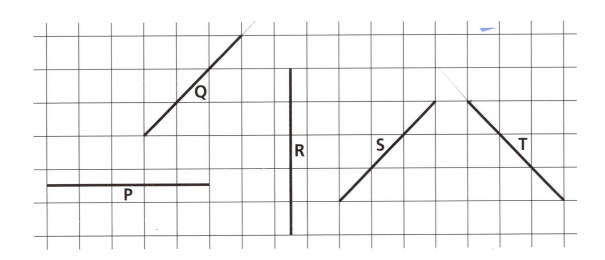

Which of these statements is correct?

A Line P is a vertical line.

B Line R is a horizontal line.

C Line Q is perpendicular to line P.

D Line S is parallel to line T.

E Line T is perpendicular to line Q.

33

These are the months of the year:

January   February   March   April   May   June   July

August   September   October   November   December

What percentage of the months begin with J?

A 12%   B 3%   C 30%   D 25%   E 20%

34

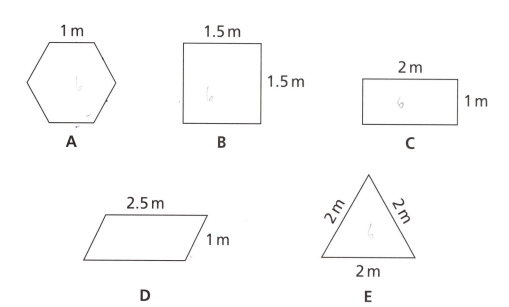

Four shapes have the same perimeter.

Which shape has a different perimeter from the others?

A A   B B   C C   D D   E E

35

On holiday, Mr Baker buys some perfume for 30 dollars and a book for 9 dollars.
He calculates that the perfume cost £20.00 and the book cost £6.00.

How much would a 15 dollar T-shirt cost in pounds?

A £9.00   B £10.00   C £11.00   D £12.00   E £13.00

36

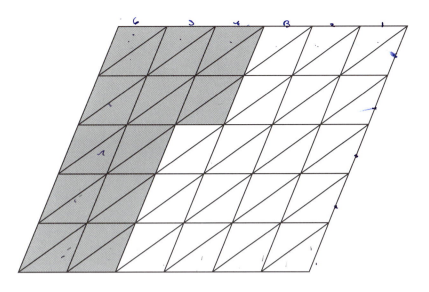

What percentage of this grid is shaded?

A 40%   **B** 24%   **C** 30%   **D** 20%   **E** 48%

37

Mrs Morgan is 5 feet 7 inches tall.

If 1 foot is 30.5 cm and 1 inch is 2.5 cm, which is closest to her height in metres?

A 1.3 m   **B** 1.4 m   **C** 2 m   **D** 1.6 m   **E** 1.7 m

---

38

Hanif will be 17 years old, 7 years from now.

How old was he 7 years ago?

A 3   **B** 6   **C** 7   **D** 8   **E** 10

---

39 This is a plan of a room.

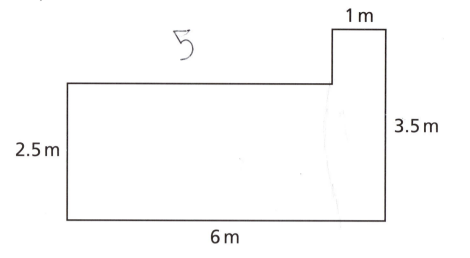

5

1 m

3.5 m

2.5 m

6 m

3,5

5

What area of carpet will be needed?

A 13 m²   B 18.5 m²   C 15 m²   D 21 m²   (E) 16 m²

40

$$81{\cdot}3 - 16{\cdot}\square\,9 =$$
$$6\,\square\cdot 81$$

Gemma's calculator displays the sum entered and the answer.
The calculator works correctly except that one digit always appears as a blank space.

What is the missing digit?

A 7   B 4   C 0   D 2   E 5

41

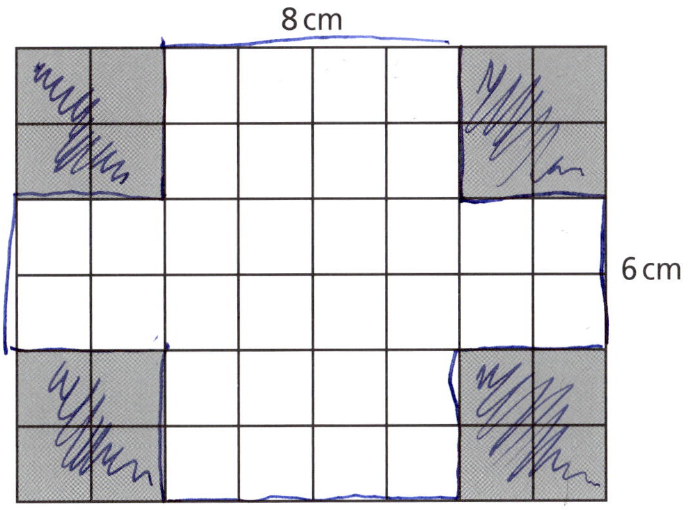

4

8 cm

6 cm   2

The shaded corners are cut out of this flat shape.
It is then folded to make a small open box.

What is the capacity of the box?

A 32 cm³   B 48 cm³   C 24 cm³   D 14 cm³   E 16 cm³

42

	Prime number	Square number	Cube number
A	25	17	1
B	21	16	7
C	29	30	8
D	27	25	16
E	29	36	27

Which row shows a prime, square and cube number in the correct order?

A A   B B   C C   D D   E E

43

Which of these numbers is closest in value to 1?

A 1.1   B 0.98   C 0.9   D 1.09   E 1.9

44

This bar chart shows the weights of a class of pupils.

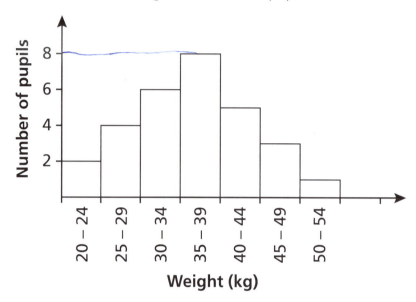

Which statement MUST be true?

A   8 children weigh between 35 kg and 39 kg.
B   8 children weigh more than 40 kg, but less than 45 kg.
C   1 child weighs exactly 55 kg.
D   No children weigh less than 21 kg.
E   5 children weigh at least 45 kg, but less than 50.5 kg.

45

Round this number to the nearest tenth.

4.13

A 4.1   B 4.3   C 4.13   D 5.13   E 4.2

46

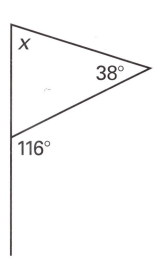

What is the size of angle *x*?

A 71°   B 26°   C 78°   D 54°   E 66°

47

Thomas walks to school each day.

One morning he recorded the types of vehicle that passed him.

He drew this chart to show the data.

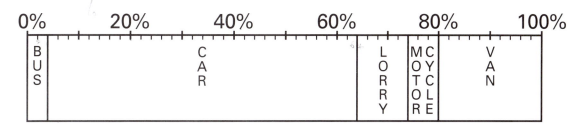

50 vehicles passed him altogether.

How many more cars were there than all other vehicles added together?

A 12   B 20   C 6   D 10   E 14

48

Marcus is working out the angles between the hands of a clock.
The clock shows twenty past twelve.

What is the smaller angle formed by the hands?

A 100° **B** 130° **C** 105° **D** 120° **E** 110°

49

What is the 5th term of this sequence?

319   193   67   …

A −175 **B** −69 **C** −185 **D** −59 **E** −101

50

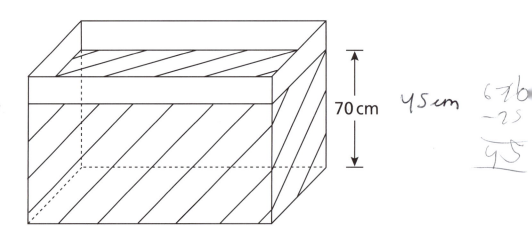

70 cm   45 cm   676
−25
45

A rectangular water tank is filled to a depth of 70 cm.
It contains 1050 litres of water.
Some water is taken out of the tank.
The water level drops by 25 cm.

How much water is left in the tank?

A 625 litres
B 375 litres
C 525 litres
D 270 litres
E 675 litres

Published by GL Assessment, 1st Floor, Vantage London, Great West Road, Brentford TW8 9AG.

Printed in China.

Code 6802 006
1(11.18) PF

Practice Paper 2

Mathematics

Read the following carefully:

1. **Do not open or turn over the page in this booklet until you are told to do so.**

2. This is a multiple-choice test in which you have to mark your answer to each question on the separate answer sheet. You should mark only one answer for each question.

3. Draw a firm line clearly through the rectangle next to your answer like this ⇔. If you make a mistake, rub it out as completely as you can and put in your new answer.

4. Be sure to keep your place on the answer sheet. Mark your answer in the box that has the same number as the question.

5. You may not be able to finish all the questions, but try to do as many as you can. If you cannot do a question, **do not waste time on it but go on to the next**. If you are not sure of an answer, choose the one you think is best.

6. You may do any rough working on a separate sheet of paper.

7. **Work as quickly and as carefully as you can.**

8. You will have **50 minutes** to do the test.

1 **Which value does the 9 in 12 097 represent?**

A 9000   B 9   C 900   D 90 000   E 90

---

2 The graph below shows the number of Christmas trees sold on 5 days at Willow Farm.

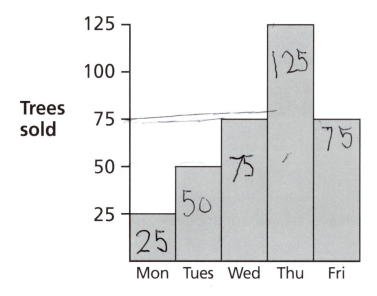

How many more trees were sold on Thursday than on Tuesday?

A 25   B 50   C 75   D 100   E 125

---

3 In a class of 32 children, three-quarters of them like painting.

3/4 of 32:24

How many children do NOT like painting?

A 8   B 6   C 4   D 9   E 12

4 Jack collected the following data during a survey of his year group.

	Favourite Message System		
	Telephone	Text	Email
Boys	10	6	28
Girls	14	?	28

(handwritten working:)
56
+24
80

28
+28
56

100
- 86

100 pupils completed the survey.

How many girls gave text as their favourite way of sending messages?

A 36   B 14   C 10   D 24   E 4

---

5 Mrs Patel spent £11.60 on 40 busy lizzie plants.

What was the cost of each plant?

A 76p   B 29p   C 40p   D £2.90   E 2.9p

---

6 A rope is 4 m 6 cm long. It is cut into two equal pieces.
(handwritten: 406)

How long is each piece?

A 2.06 m   B 2.30 m   C 2.46 m   D 0.23 m   E 2.03 m

---

7 Look at this table showing the performance of the school hockey team.

Year	Won	Lost	Drawn
2014	7	6	4
2015	3	7	2
2016	8	4	5

How many matches in total did the team not win?

A 18   B 17   C 11   D 29   E 28

8 Which of these words has a vertical line of symmetry?

DID

DAB

HAD

MUM

MUD

A DID   **B** DAB   **C** HAD   **D** MUM   **E** MUD

---

9 Year 6 are all going on a day trip to France.
There are 33 children in Year 6 and the trip costs £25 each.

How much money must be collected in total from the children?

A £58   **B** £82.50   **C** £150   **D** £580   **E** £825

33
×25
16 5
66 0
82 5

---

10 This grid shows a car park.

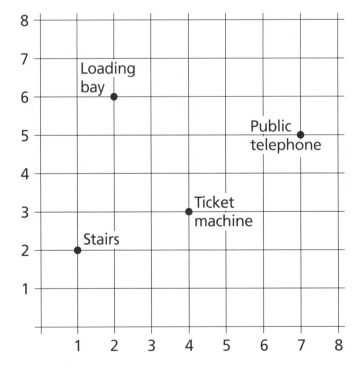

Where is the ticket machine?

A (4 , 3)   **B** (2 , 4)   **C** (3 , 4)   **D** (4 , 2)   **E** (2 , 6)

11 Our school magazine has 56 pages.

$\frac{2}{7}$ of the pages contain typing errors.

$\frac{2}{7}$ of 56 = 16

How many pages contain typing errors?

A 14   B 9   C 16   D 27   E 15

---

12 A rectangle has an area of 54 cm².

$\begin{array}{r} 9\overset{\scriptstyle 4}{5}4 \\ -\ 36 \\ \hline 18 \end{array}$

If two of the sides are both 6 cm long, what is the length of each of the other two sides?

A 6 cm   B 5.4 cm   C 9 cm   D 5 cm   E 8 cm

---

13 This machine divides by 5 and then multiplies by 3.

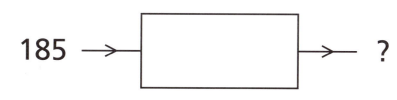

185 →   → ?

$\begin{array}{r} 037 \\ 5\overline{)1^18^35} \end{array}$

$\begin{array}{r} 2 \\ 37 \\ \times\ 3 \\ \hline 111 \end{array}$

Which number comes out?

A 29   B 37   C 111   D 85   E 115

---

14 Look at the grid in which there are some empty squares.

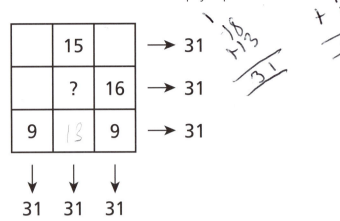

When every square is filled in, each row and each column adds up to 31.

Which number should be in the square with the question mark?

A 13   **B** 6   **C** 12   **D** 3   **E** 10

---

15 **What is this number rounded to the nearest tenth:**

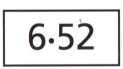

A 6.5   **B** 6.6   **C** 6.52   **D** 6.53   **E** 6.2

---

16 A medium-sized teapot holds just enough for four cups of tea.

Which volume is most likely to be true for the teapot?

A 2 litres   **B** 0.3 litres   **C** 300 ml   **D** 4 litres   **E** 800 ml

---

17 In five years' time, Peter's cat will be 12 years old.

How old was his cat 6 years ago?

A 13   **B** 23   **C** 7   **D** 5   **E** 1

---

18 Sanjay let me finish his box of mints.
He had eaten ⅝ of them.

If 36 mints were left for me, how many had Sanjay eaten?

A 60   B 58   C 68   D 36   E 56

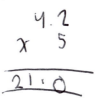
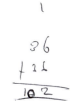

19 Two coaches are booked for the school trip.
The first coach seats 56 passengers, and the second 43.
8 adults, 41 boys and 38 girls are going on the trip.

How many spare seats will there be?

A 11   B 48   C 35   D 12   E 20

20 John and his sister Debra held a cake sale at their school to raise money for charity.
They sold 48 large cakes at 10p each and 65 small cakes at 5p each.

How much money did they make at their sale?

A £8.05   B £37.30   C £11.30   D £5.65   E £80.50

21

Here is the plan of a room.

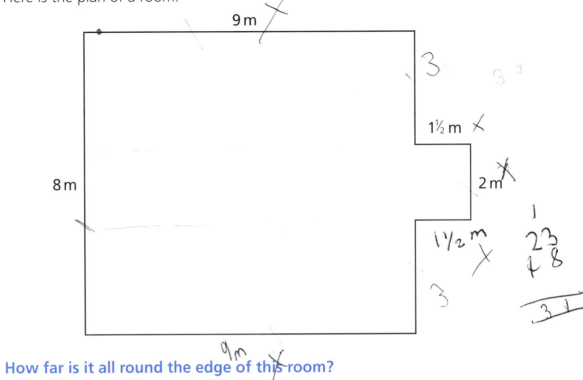

How far is it all round the edge of this room?

A 37 m   **B** 72 m   **C** 75 m   **D** 41 m   **E** 33 m

22

Which shape has more than two lines of symmetry?

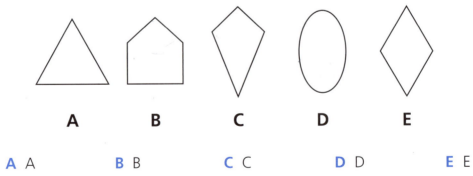

A   **B**   **C**   **D**   **E**

A A   **B** B   **C** C   **D** D   **E** E

23

Which number is exactly divisible by 2 and 8?

A 18   **B** 28   **C** 32   **D** 42   **E** 52

24

The Crystal 5 cinema charges £3.50 entrance for adults and £3 for children.
Popcorn is £1.50 for a large bag and £1.25 for a small bag.

What is the total cost for Mr and Mrs Jenkins to take their two children to the cinema if each adult has a large bag of popcorn and each child has a small bag?

A £12.50   B £16.25   C £9.25   D £18.50   E £15.00

25

You multiply a number by 3.
The answer is doubled then divided by 6.
The result is 5.

What number did you start with?

A 5   B 6   C 3   D 30   E 15

26

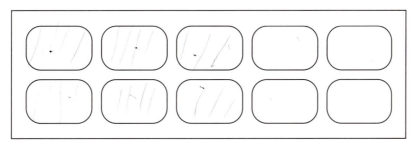

Kim uses six ice cubes in drinks for her friends.

What percentage of the ice cubes is left?

A 60%   B 50%   C 40%   D 30%   E 20%

---

27 Mr Sohal is looking at the effect of temperature.
He repeats the same experiment several times.
Each time, the temperature is 4 °C cooler than the previous time.
He did the first experiment at 25 °C.

At what temperature did he carry out his eighth experiment?

A −3 °C   B 0 °C   C −7 °C   D 1 °C   E −5 °C

---

28 Sarah's mum buys her a new school skirt in a sale at half price.
The original cost of the skirt was £9.50.

How much change does Sarah's mum get from her £10 note?

A 25p   B 50p   C £4.50   D £4.75   E £5.25

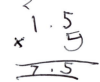

---

29 Five parking spaces are being marked out along the roadside.
An average car is 4 m long.

Allowing an extra 1.5 m per car for driving into the space, roughly how long should the spaces be altogether?

A 0.25 km   B 28 m   C 35 m   D 25 m   E 0.20 km

27.5

30

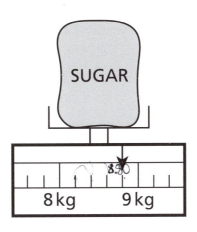

SUGAR

8 kg   9 kg

The arrow shows how much the sack of sugar weighs.

If another 600 g of sugar is added, what will the total weight be?

A 9.4 kg   B 9.0 kg   C 9.2 kg   D 9.6 kg   E 8.6 kg

31

Jasmina is trying to calculate the area of this shape. She has spotted that she can make it into a rectangle and has drawn this onto her diagram.

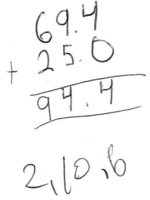

5 cm

2.7 cm   3 cm

1 cm

Calculate the area of this shape.

A 15 cm²   B 13.5 cm²   C 12.05 cm²   D 17.7 cm²   E 16 cm²

32 Jamal has a square card.
He marks the middle of one side.
He cuts off the small triangles shown.

What type of triangle is Jamal left with?

A equilateral   B right-angled   C scalene   D obtuse-angled   E isosceles

---

33 At Sally's school, there are 860 children.
95% like chips.

How many children don't like chips?

A 43   B 95   C 765   D 817   E 5

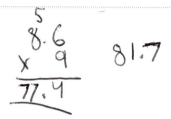

---

34 Class 5 are recording the outside temperature every morning and afternoon.
On Tuesday morning, Nina read the temperature.

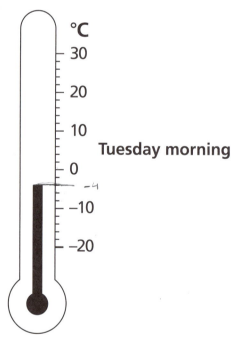

Tuesday morning

During the day, the temperature rose 7 °C.

What was the temperature in the afternoon?

A 7 °C   B 10 °C   C 5 °C   D 3 °C   E 8 °C

---

35 29 children were asked whether they like swimming, running and cycling. Their answers are shown in this diagram:

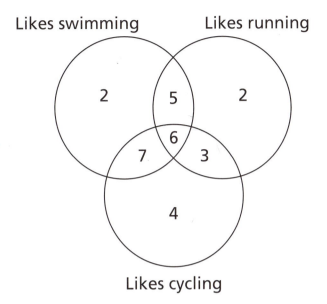

How many children like both running and cycling, but NOT swimming?

A 7   B 3   C 6   D 5   E 4

36

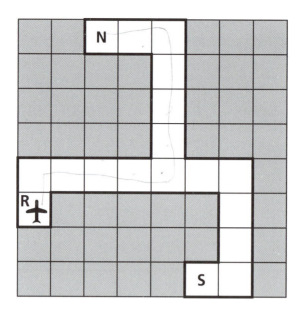

At the airport, Ground Control must guide a plane from the end of the runway, point R, to the North terminal, point N.

The plane can only move FORWARD, TURN LEFT 90° or TURN RIGHT 90°.

Which set of instructions will guide the plane from the runway (R) to the North terminal (N)?

A   FORWARD 1, TURN RIGHT 90°, FORWARD 6, TURN RIGHT 90°, FORWARD 3, TURN RIGHT 90°, FORWARD 1.

B   FORWARD 1, TURN RIGHT 90°, FORWARD 4, TURN LEFT 90°, FORWARD 4, TURN LEFT 90°, FORWARD 2.

C   FORWARD 1, TURN LEFT 90°, FORWARD 4, TURN LEFT 90°, FORWARD 4, TURN RIGHT 90°, FORWARD 2.

D   FORWARD 1, TURN RIGHT 90°, FORWARD 6, TURN LEFT 90°, FORWARD 3, TURN RIGHT 90°, FORWARD 1.

E   FORWARD 1, TURN RIGHT 90°, FORWARD 4, TURN RIGHT 90°, FORWARD 4, TURN LEFT 90°, FORWARD 2.

37

The school clock is put right on Monday at 11.00 a.m.

At 11.00 a.m. on Tuesday it gives the time as 11.02 a.m.

How much time does the clock gain every hour?

A 1 minute   B 15 seconds   C 5 seconds   D 2 minutes   E 10 seconds

38 **Which answer describes the three triangles below in order from left to right?**

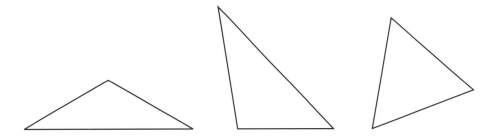

    A scalene, isosceles, equilateral
    B isosceles, scalene, equilateral
    C equilateral, scalene, isosceles
    D scalene, equilateral, isosceles
    E equilateral, isosceles, scalene

39

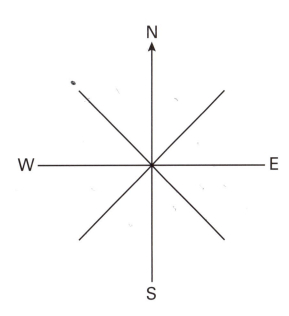

Anita is facing NW.
She then turns anti-clockwise through 585°.

Which direction does she now face?

    A E   **B** N   **C** NE   **D** SE   **E** S

40

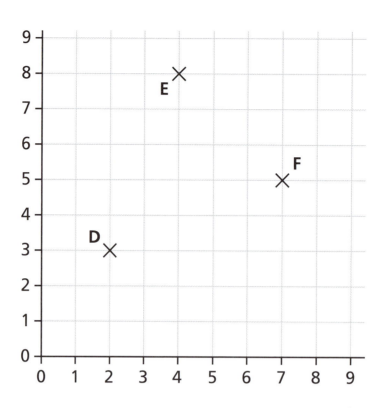

What are the coordinates of D, E and F?

A D (3 , 2) E (8 , 4) F (5 , 7)

B D (2 , 3) E (4 , 8) F (7 , 5)

C D (2 , 3) E (4 , 7) F (7 , 5)

D D (3 , 2) E (7 , 5) F (4 , 8)

E D (3 , 2) E (4 , 8) F (5 , 7)

---

41 **Which one of these gives the answer 30?**

A 25% of 80 -20

B $\frac{2}{5}$ of 75 - 30

C $\frac{3}{4}$ of 45

D 70% of 40

E 40% of 60

42 Lollipops cost the same as sherbet dips.
Sherbet dips cost twice as much as jelly rings.
Four of the following cost the same.

Which does not cost the same as the rest?

A 3 sherbet dips, 2 jelly rings, 1 lollipop
B 2 lollipops, 2 sherbet dips, 2 jelly rings
C 3 sherbet dips, 2 lollipops
D 2 lollipops, 4 jelly rings, 2 sherbet dips
E 1 lollipop, 6 jelly rings, 1 sherbet dip

43 Rajiv draws a quadrilateral with only one pair of equal angles and only one line of reflective symmetry.

What is the name of this quadrilateral?

A square   B rectangle   C kite   D rhombus   E trapezium

44 This bar chart shows how many times a class of children hit a target with a set of ten beanbags.

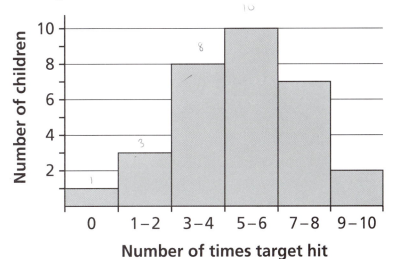

How many children hit the target fewer than 7 times?

A 22   B 29   C 12   D 21   E 10

45 Which one of these is closest to 888.88 + 88.88 + 8.88 + 0.88?

A 975   B 1000   C 998   D 990   E 968

46 On day 1, 4 people are sent an email.
On day 2, each of the 4 send it to 4 more people, and so on.
Each person sends the email just once.

How many people have received the email by day 4?

A 64   B 256   C 84   D 340   E 240

47 An isosceles triangle has angles X, Y and Z.
Angle X measures 55°.
Angles X and Y differ by 15°.

What is the size of angle Z?

A 15°   B 40°   C 55°   D 70°   E 80°

48

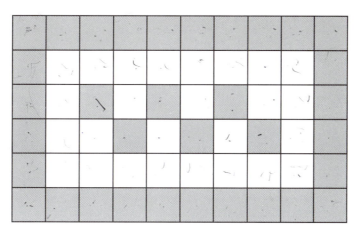

Each of these grey and white carpet tiles measures 50 cm × 50 cm.

What is the total area covered by the grey carpet tiles, in square metres?

A 60 m²   **B** 30 m²   **C** 34 m²   **D** 17 m²   **E** 8.5 m²

49

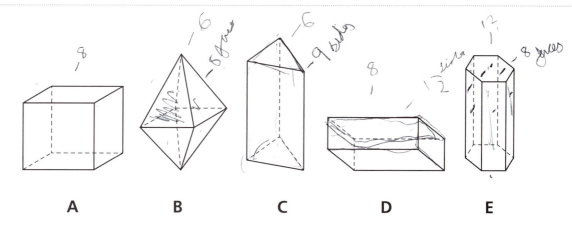

    A   **B**   **C**   **D**   **E**

Which of the above solids has more faces than vertices?

A A   **B** B   **C** C   **D** D   **E** E

50

Amul divided a whole number less than 200 by a whole number greater than 15. The result was a whole number.

What is the largest possible result of Amul's division?

A 13   **B** 12   **C** 14   **D** 11   **E** 15

Published by GL Assessment, 1st Floor, Vantage London, Great West Road, Brentford TW8 9AG.

Printed in China.

Code 6802 007
1(11.18) PF

Practice Paper 3

Mathematics

Read the following carefully:

1. **Do not open or turn over the page in this booklet until you are told to do so.**

2. This is a multiple-choice test in which you have to mark your answer to each question on the separate answer sheet. You should mark only one answer for each question.

3. Draw a firm line clearly through the rectangle next to your answer like this ⟺. If you make a mistake, rub it out as completely as you can and put in your new answer.

4. Be sure to keep your place on the answer sheet. Mark your answer in the box that has the same number as the question.

5. You may not be able to finish all the questions, but try to do as many as you can. If you cannot do a question, **do not waste time on it but go on to the next**. If you are not sure of an answer, choose the one you think is best.

6. You may do any rough working on a separate sheet of paper.

7. **Work as quickly and as carefully as you can.**

8. You will have **50 minutes** to do the test.

1

12 345

The 2 in this number is worth 2000.

What is the 3 worth?

A 3000   **B** 30   **C** 12 300   **D** 3   **E** 300

2

This graph shows the number of computer games sold by a shop in four weeks.

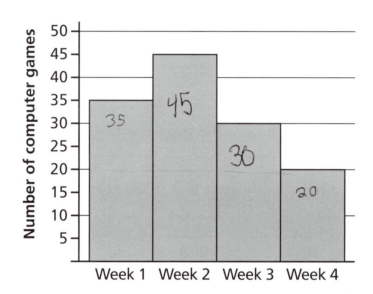

How many more computer games were sold in Week 1 than in Week 4?

A 3   **B** 15   **C** 10   **D** 25   **E** 30

3

Twenty-four thousand seven hundred and six.

Which answer shows this written as a number?

A 24 706   **B** 2476   **C** 24 760   **D** 2470.6   **E** 24 700.6

---

4 How many fives are there in 870?

A 87   B 169   C 435   D 174   E 56

---

5 Which number has the smallest value?

A 1.01   B 0.99   C 0.02   D 1.25   E 0.5

---

6 Claire packed her rucksack for a day's hike in the country.
It contained a flask of hot tea, some sandwiches, two apples, a banana and a bar of chocolate.
She also packed some waterproof clothes.

How much is the rucksack likely to weigh?

A 3 kg   B 300 g   C 30 kg   D 300 kg   E 3 g

---

7 This machine multiplies by 3 and then subtracts 6.

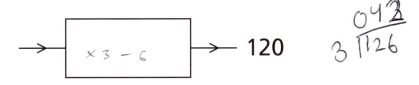

Which number has been put in?

A 84   B 42   C 82   D 48   E 36

8

In a concert hall, there are 592 seats.
306 tickets are sold in advance.
178 tickets are sold at the door.

$$\begin{array}{r} 1 \\ 306 \\ + 178 \\ \hline 484 \end{array} \qquad \begin{array}{r} 8 \\ 5\cancel{9}2 \\ - 484 \\ \hline 108 \end{array}$$

How many empty chairs are there during the concert?

A 286 **B** 108 **C** 464 **D** 180 **E** 414

9

There are 12 eggs in a dozen.

How many eggs are there in four and a half dozen?

A 45 **B** 48 **C** 50 **D** 60 **E** 54

10

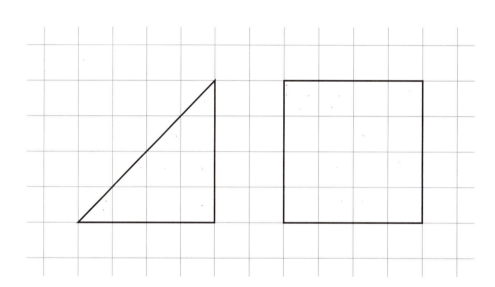

In this diagram, one small square represents 1 cm².

What is the difference in area between these two shapes?

A 20 cm² **B** 16 cm² **C** 8 cm² **D** 2 cm² **E** 4 cm²

11 Gemma and Li did a survey on favourite pizza toppings.

Favourite Pizza Toppings	
Key: ◯ stands for 6 children	
◗ stands for 3 children	
Cheese and tomato	◯◯◯◯ 24
Tuna and sweetcorn	◯◯◯◯◗ 27
Hot and spicy pepperoni	◯◯ 12
Tomato, mushroom and onion	◯◯◗ 15
Hawaiian pineapple	◯◯◯◗ 21

How many children liked tuna and sweetcorn best?

A 27   B 5   C 9   D 4½   E 24

12 Today's temperature is 3 °C.
Yesterday, it was −4 °C.

What is the difference between these two temperatures?

A 1 °C   B −1 °C   C 7 °C   D −7 °C   E −4 °C

13

Which answer has three numbers that are all cube numbers?

A 8, 16, 32

B 8, 27, 64

C 16, 32, 64

D 9, 27, 64

E 5, 25, 125

14

Which fraction has the largest value?

A ½   B ¾ ²/₃   C ⅝ ⁴/₅   D ¹⁰/₁₂ ⁶/₁₂   E ⁴/₆ ³/₆

15

Liam halves his dad's age.
He then adds 7.
The result is 26.

19
x 2
38

How old is his dad?

A 38   B 19   C 33   D 21   E 39

16

Which of these words has a vertical line of symmetry?

TOT

ON

BIB

OF

BE

A TOT   B ON   C BIB   D OF   E BE

17

There are 30 pupils in a class.

$\frac{1}{5}$ go home for lunch.

$\frac{2}{5}$ buy a school lunch.

The rest bring sandwiches.

$\frac{1}{5}$ of $30 = 6$

$\frac{2}{5}$ of $30 = 12$

How many pupils bring sandwiches?

A 6   **B** 18   **C** 12   **D** 2   **E** 5

18

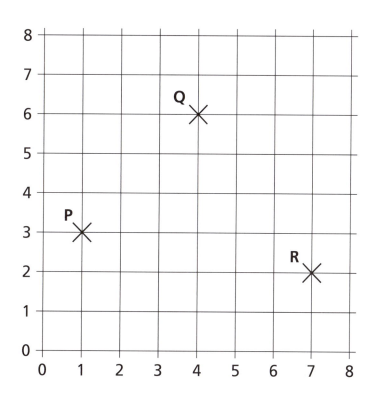

What are the coordinates of P, Q and R?

A P (3 , 1)   Q (6 , 4)   R (2 , 7)

B P (1 , 2)   Q (4 , 6)   R (7 , 1)

C P (1 , 3)   Q (4 , 6)   R (7 , 2)

D P (1 , 3)   Q (7 , 2)   R (4 , 6)

E P (1 , 3)   Q (4 , 6)   R (2 , 7)

19 The kitchen clock says 5 o'clock.

What is the smaller angle between the clock hands?

A 135°   B 155°   C 150°   D 165°   E 130°

20

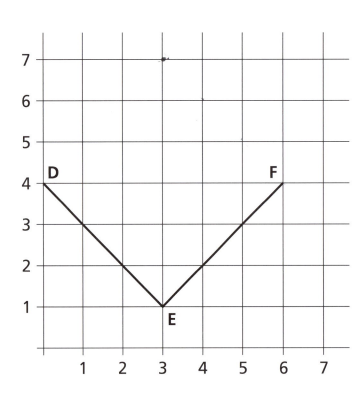

When point G is added, DEFG is a square.

What are the coordinates of point G?

A (7 , 3)   B (4 , 6)   C (2 , 7)   D (3 , 7)   E (4 , 7)

21 The Hassan family have two pints of milk delivered every day.
Milk costs 41p for a pint.

What is the Hassan family's weekly milk bill?

A £5.60   B £2.05   C £6.04   D £4.92   E £5.74

22 This graph converts kilometres to miles.

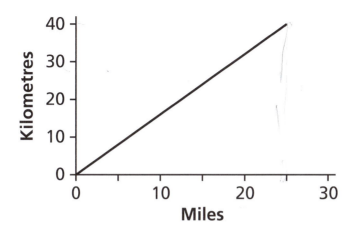

How many miles are in 400 km?

A 250 miles

B 25 miles

C 205 miles

D 800 miles

E 40 miles

---

23 David has keyboard lessons which cost £20.50 each week.
He has three 12-week terms.

What is the total cost of his lessons in a year?

A £492   B £205   C £287   D £246   E £738

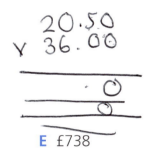

24 The diagram below shows part of a shape and two of its lines of symmetry.

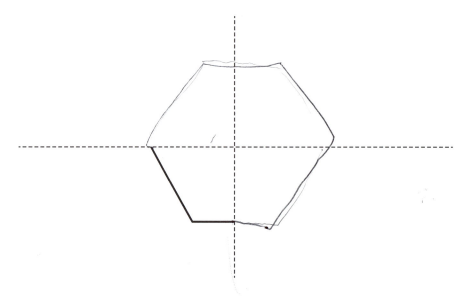

What is the name of the complete shape?

A kite ✗

B regular pentagon ✗

C regular hexagon

D rhombus ✗

E regular octagon

25

3 1 2
9̶8̶.2̶5̶
×   4
3̶7̶3̶.00

Furniture	
Sofa:	£758.49
Armchair:	£245.00
Dining table:	£376.65
Dining chair:	£98.25

2 11 1
758.49
490.00
376.65
+ 373.00
1998.14

= 1140 +

Mr Lee buys one sofa, two armchairs, one dining table and four dining chairs.

What is the total cost of this furniture?

A £1478.39   B £1723.39   C £1773.14   D £1878.39   E £2018.14

26

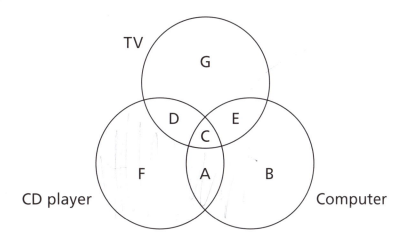

The three circles represent the children in a class who have TVs, CD players and computers.

Which area shows the children who do NOT have a TV?

A B + A + F

B G − B − F

C F + C + B

D A + B + D

E F + A + B + A

27 **How many millimetres is 0.08 kilometres?**

A 8 mm   B 80 mm   C 800 mm   D 8000 mm   E 80 000 mm

28

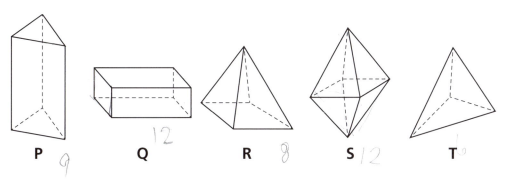

P   Q   R   S   T

Which two solids have the same number of edges?

A P and R   B Q and S   C R and T   D P and S   E P and Q

29

Ravi earns £35.50 from his weekly paper round.
He is paid at the end of each week.

If he saves all the money, how many weeks must he work before he can buy a mobile phone costing £150?

A 5   B 6   C 7   D 8   E 9

30

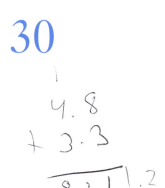

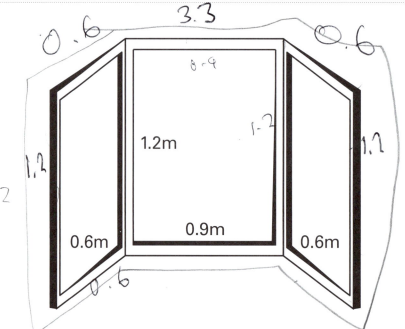

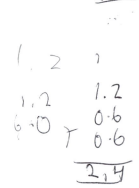

A bay window is made up of one rectangular section with a height of 1.2 m and a width of 0.9 m, and two rectangular sections each with a height of 1.2 m and a width of 0.6 m.

What is the perimeter of the bay window in metres?

A 25.2 m   B 6.6 m   C 9.0 m   D 11.4 m   E 5.4 m

31

Out of a class of 36 children, 17 have younger brothers and sisters.

Approximately what proportion is this?

A ½   B ⅔   C ¼   D ⅗   E ⅜

32 This magic grid contains a number sequence which increases in steps.

84	96	108
96	108	120
108	120	?

What is the missing number?

A 108   **B** 132   **C** 96   **D** 120   **E** 84

33

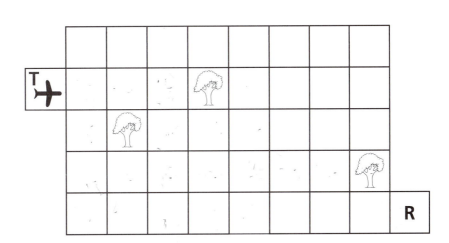

At the airport, Ground Control must guide a plane from point T to the beginning of the runway, R, ready to take off, avoiding any trees on the way.

The plane can only move FORWARD, TURN LEFT 90° or TURN RIGHT 90°.

Which set of instructions will guide the plane to the runway avoiding any trees?

A FORWARD 3, RIGHT 90°, FORWARD 2, LEFT 90°, FORWARD 5.

B FORWARD 1, LEFT 90°, FORWARD 2, RIGHT 90°, FORWARD 7.

C FORWARD 3, RIGHT 90°, FORWARD 3, LEFT 90°, FORWARD 6.

D FORWARD 1, RIGHT 90°, FORWARD 2, LEFT 90°, FORWARD 7.

E FORWARD 3, LEFT 90°, FORWARD 3, LEFT 90°, FORWARD 6.

34

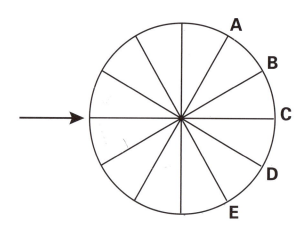

This circle is divided into 12 equal sectors.
It is rotated 150° anticlockwise about its centre.

To which point on the circle is the arrow now pointing?

A A   **B** B   **C** C   **D** D   **E** E

---

35   **Which fraction is equivalent to $^{20}/_{32}$?**

A $^5/_8$ **B** $^{12}/_{16}$ **C** $^4/_{10}$ **D** $^6/_8$ **E** $^8/_5$

---

36   **Work out the name of this 2D shape from the clues:**

1. It has four sides.
2. The diagonals do **not** cross at right angles.
3. All interior angles are right angles.

A   rectangle
B   trapezium
C   kite
D   rhombus
E   square

37

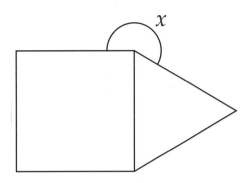

The above shape is made from a square and an equilateral triangle.

What is the size of angle x?

A 90°   B 150°   C 180°   D 210°   E 270°

38

An examiner marks 300 exam papers.
There are 86 questions in each paper.

300
×86

1800
2700
25800

How many questions does she mark altogether?

A 2580   B 28500   C 386   D 258   E 25800

39

120

What fraction of 2 hours is 45 minutes?

A ²⁄₃   B ⁶⁄₈   C ²⁄₄₅   D ³⁄₄   E ³⁄₈

40

Mr Jones is training for the London marathon.
He runs 8 kilometres every weekday and twice as far on Saturday and on Sunday.

How far does he run in one week?

A 40 km   B 56 km   C 72 km   D 88 km   E 104 km

41

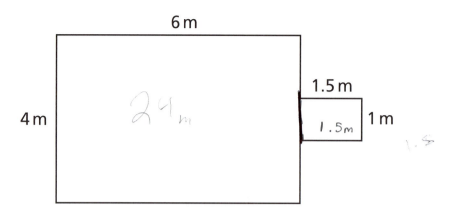

6 m

4 m   24 m

1.5 m

1.5m   1 m

1.5

This is a plan of a hallway.

What area of carpet will be needed to completely cover the hallway?

A 24 m²   **B** 30 m²   **C** 29 m²   **D** 25.5 m²   **E** 22.5 m²

42 There are 32 pupils in Class 6M.

Mrs Moore checked class attendance across one week.

The bar chart shows the number of pupils who were absent each day.

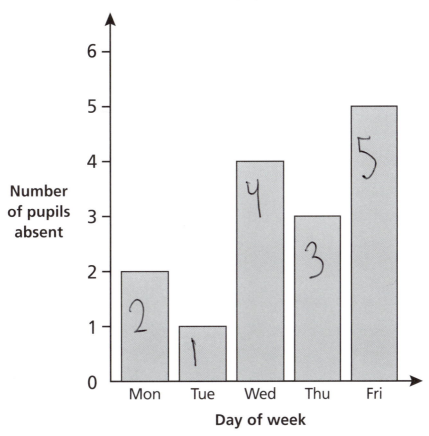

Which one of these statements MUST be true?

A Only 17 pupils attended school every day of the week.

B 15 different pupils were absent during the week.

C Between 27 and 31 pupils attended every day of the week.

D 27 pupils attended school every day of the week.

E Only 5 pupils were absent during the week.

43

A Greek holiday costs £375 per person.
There is a £60 reduction for each child.

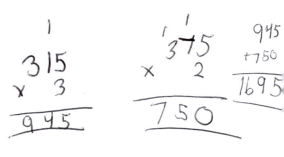

How much would it cost for Mr and Mrs Johnson to go on the holiday and take their three children with them?

A £1380   **B** £1320   **C** £1815   **D** £1695   **E** £1440

44

Ben drew this right-angled triangle on a square grid.

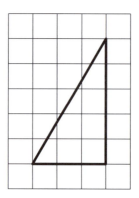

Libby joined up three of the points on the square coordinate grid below to draw a triangle that is exactly the same size and shape as Ben's.

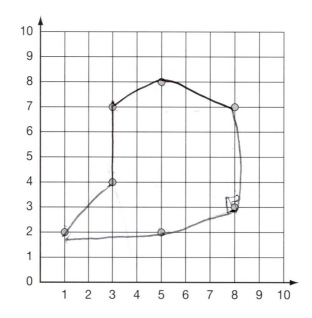

What are the coordinates of the right-angled corner of Libby's triangle?

A (3 , 4)   **B** (3 , 7)   **C** (5 , 2)   **D** (8 , 3)   **E** (8 , 7)

45 The price of a game in the local toyshop has been reduced by 20%.
The original price was £9.50.

9.5
+9.5
19.0

How much is it now?

A £1.90   B £7.50   C £7.60   D £8.55   E £9.30

---

46 Shape S is made from four regular hexagons. T is an equilateral triangle.

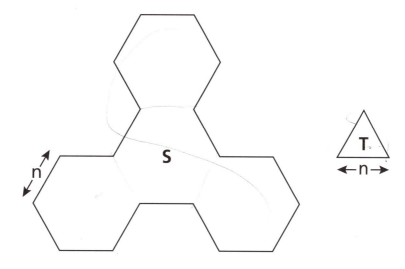

How many times will shape T fit into shape S?

A 6   B 18   C 20   D 24   E 30

---

47   Mr Cooper compares the price of the same window blinds at five shops.

Shop	Cost
A	50% off £89
B	25% off £60
C	£49
D	4 for £179
E	3 for £140

(handwritten: 5 44.50)
(handwritten: 45)
(handwritten: 49)
(handwritten: 44.75)
(handwritten: 46.60)

Which shop gives the cheapest cost per blind?

A A   **B** B   **C** C   **D** D   **E** E

---

48   **Which of these areas is the same as 0.5 m²?**

A 50 cm²   **B** 500 cm²   **C** 5000 cm²   **D** 2500 cm²   **E** 250 cm²

49

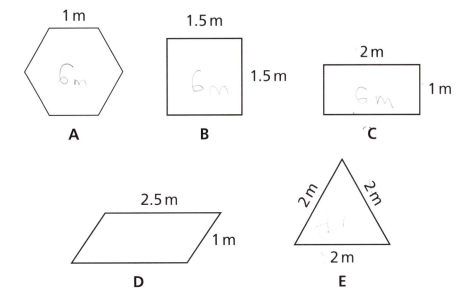

Four shapes have the same perimeter.

Which shape has a different perimeter from the others?

A A   **B** B   **C** C   **D** D   **E** E

50

Joshua and Emma each start to grow a plant on the same day.
After one week, both plants are 5 centimetres tall.
During the next three weeks Joshua's plant grows 4 centimetres per week and
Emma's grows 4.5 centimetres per week.

When the plants are four weeks old, how much taller is Emma's plant than Joshua's in centimetres?

A 6.0 cm   **B** 5.5 cm   **C** 4.0 cm   **D** 2.0 cm   **E** 1.5 cm

Published by GL Assessment, 1st Floor, Vantage London, Great West Road, Brentford TW8 9AG.

Printed in China.

Code 6802 008
1(11.18) PF